My Coolest Shirt

Also by W.T. Pfefferle:

The Meager Life and Modest Times of Pop Thorndale
Writing That Matters
Poets on Place

My Coolest Shirt

poems by

W.T. Pfefferle

THE WORD WORKS
WASHINGTON DC

Acknowledgments:

The Advocate: "Winter Afternoon."
Alternative Press Magazine: "Laramie."
Antioch Review: "Second Marriage."
The Café Review: "A Postcard to the Northeast."
Dream International Quarterly: "Swimming."
Exit 13: "New Mexico."
Hayden's Ferry Review: "Satellites."
The Messenger: "Summer with the Artist."
Mississippi Review: "Hero."
Nimrod: "Losing Clare."
North American Review: "Map Reading."
Santa Fe Online—Poetry Forum: "Driving"
     and "Night Vision."
Verse Libre Quarterly: "Cigarette," "Driveways,"
     and "Careful."
Virginia Quarterly Review: "Bad History."
Zuzu's Petals: "Porch Swing."

CONTENTS

Salvation

This place is cool.
This is my coolest shirt.

Let me see what I can salvage
from past scattered moments.

I once believed I was a dream.
A felt hat worn by a rakish angel.

But what I thought was salvation
was really only car wrecks.

Lucky for me, I believe in redemption,
in sins forgiven.

A balloon rising over sandy mountains,
a paper heart cut with crooked scissors.

Something that keeps me warm,
on this, the coolest day of the year.

Hero

Things weren't always like this.
There was furniture here once,
and I had a lot of it.

Couch, chair.
Same coloring, same pattern.
A coffee table.

And all the bedroom stuff,
queen size, lamp,
the works.

But you know how that is,
and you know what a room looks like
without things.

I used to be her hero.
I used to drive
a big car.

I used to know something about stars,
and planets and comets,
and we used to go out there at night to look up.

There was something we used to say back then,
and sometimes when I'm here
wondering about my furniture,

sometimes when I'm here,
in what used to be a living
room.

I can sometimes remember what it was.

Losing Clare

I prayed for a foggy morning,
one that would somehow shield me
from the inevitable.

A little plane can't leave this island in the fog.
Even a wind will change schedules.
It happens all the time.

All night I stood on the shore,
prayed for clouds,
made deals with the angels.

When the sun came up the next morning,
it was clear.
The water lapped lazily.

I talked about some bad movie, some bad seafood,
and you ticked off in your head
all the reasons you were leaving.

Perfect sunny morning and you wore
tortoise shell sunglasses I had paid too much for
years and years before.

Later, on the beach,
I looked up and cursed the clouds
that arrived too late.

I drank white whiskey right out of the bottle,
and pretended you would be emerging soon
from a cabana behind me.

Ready to lead me back to where we'd been.

My Bad Girlfriend Worries About Me

She calls me Punky, like the TV show.
Although I don't like it.

She has an extra set of my keys
that she believes she will use
as tools of vengeance
when we finally break up.

At movies she "harrumphs" loudly,
and sticks her feet over the row ahead.
She gives the asst. manager a big bored sigh
when he comes flashlighting through.

(I love her though, of course,
like I love highways.)
She smokes my cigarettes halfway
and then stubs them out.

She wolfs my cheeseburger.
She wonders if I could be more bold,
and more thin.
She'd prefer either of those.

She calls me Punky now,
even when we're not alone.

Bad History

Columbus liked to wear giant plumed hats
and was fond of a woman he later sold for beads.

The Civil War started sometime in an early morning rain
and continues to this day.

Nietzsche said that all that glistens is gold.
Chaucer told tales of lovers without conscience.

The houses in heaven have several rooms.
God ran off Lucifer because of my pride.

I wrote a bad check to buy the ring,
and later she sold it to pay for the U-Haul.

The railway opened the country,
the automobile dispersed the populace.

The television was invented in the 1930s,
and then Netta threw it down the stairs

of the Sunflower apartment building,
on a day that looked like rain,

but when no rain came.

Lessons from Napoleon

The girls on television are talking about infidelity.
We whisper things back at them.

Netta's first husband was a scoundrel.
That's an actual word I've heard her use.

Napoleon, I say, was buried in a coffin
made for a child.

She mixes something red in margarita glasses.
The afternoon stretches like a hamstring.

Netta says Barbara Eden was on television yesterday.
She still has a flat belly.

Napoleon was married to a redhead.
But he loved her all the same.

Netta takes off her sweater and tosses it to the rug.
I see a stack of holiday photos on the coffee table.

They were happy and laughing.
Napoleon found love, too.

Netta tells me it's almost 5:30,
but nobody is moving.

Satellites

We're racing across Charles on a cloudy day,
wind pressing newspaper to store windows,
people in gray and black raincoats shoot past
in clumps of threes and fours.

Now we're standing on a patch of beach by an ocean
that we've never seen before,
and she's throwing pieces of broken shells
as far as she can into the water.

We're on a highway in Wyoming
and she's rolling the spare tire toward me.
We watch it roll down the embankment,
moving quickly away from us.

In an open field outside Wichita,
we spot shooting stars in darkening sky.
I'm wishing on them.
747s, Clare says. Russian satellites.

She tells me things change.
She turns it like a lock.

Sailing

We shoot across the small bay,
making lines in the water like streams of light.

We're losing wind, you say,
and I look back at the shore,

white patches above the horizon,
sand, flashes of lights, glare of traffic

on the beach highway.
I dream of us in some desert state,

throwing coins into a crevice,
shooting across the sand,

fighting the desert winds,
fighting the desert storms.

I hear a calliope from my childhood
squealing its song like madness.

I open my eyes and watch the tip of the mast
cut swaths in a cobalt sky.

We eat in a restaurant later.
You want to talk about the future.

Instead I draw on my napkin,
canyons, ferris wheels, and satellites.

House Painting

In darkening afternoon light, I find remembrances
of another house. That one big and musty.
Walls the color of cranberry and avocado.

We have pictures of that house and others too.
They stagger along a poorly
drawn imaginary line on one wall.

I'm hearing door slams from Portland,
and feeling the draft from a window in Illinois.
Smelling the *menudo* across an open alley in Texas.

The whole house is painted to fade walls,
so carpet and ceilings wash together.
A man could paint this whole place in a day.

Maybe the color of this latest can of Pepsi.
Maybe a lipstick smear across the dining room,
a turned-over blush in the foyer, new skin for everything.

We could paint.
We could cover it all in drop cloths,
paint blind with eyes closed.

Exhausted at the finish,
cleaned up at the end of day.
Let night's color hide it till morning.

Marvel at sunrise's unveiling.

Summer in Cali.

She reports on triple digits
and the death of her tomatoes.
Corn stalks exploding. Apricots falling,
bursting open from the heat.

My summer is hundreds of miles north,
with temperate rains
and cloudy, foggy mornings
when I write her letters.
Some I send. Some I rip into clean strips
and drop into a wastepaper basket.

"When things get better," Netta writes,
"I'll send you the plane fare.
Enough for a one way, some smokes,
and a hotel room for both of us."
"When the weather breaks," I say,
"I'll come down myself."

I've got two months, maybe.
Before fall, I mean.

In two months I'll need a better story.

My Bad Girlfriend on a Sunday

She says she's lost my phone.

She leaves me fifty dollar grocery lists
with a ten dollar bill.

On weekends she gets up early,
vacuums around the bed.

On Sundays she insists we pray,
but not to God.

She tells a neighbor that I wish I had his flat belly.

She can be counted on to take the can to the curb,
but to never, ever, bring it back.

My bad girlfriend jingles when I jangle.

Laramie

We've found a green hotel.
Carry me across, she says.

She's pretending.

Drop her on the bed,
but she's already up,
hopping around the room,
letting her hair fly,
white socks on red bedspread.

When it is dark we look out the window.
Big Sky country, she says.

I don't tell her.
She doesn't know the difference.

She smokes her Marlboros,
warming her hands around them,
while I sleep underneath the Indian pictures.

Press 6 for wake up.

In the morning I take the car to a 7-Eleven for gas.
As I drive back toward the hotel,
I remember why I married her.
And I forget why we got divorced.

Outside the hotel,
she is standing by a Coke machine,
waiting on the curb.

She's swinging her arms,
balancing.

Horizons

We're sitting in chairs,
listening to records that we've been playing all night.

It's raining outside, the streets look wet, frosted,
cars shoot across them, skittering like cans.

I'm wasting away in a downward spiral of parking tickets,
legal fees, fried chicken, moving boxes, and packing tape.

I see a face in the mirror that I don't recognize.
Dust is chasing dust, the phone's been lost for weeks.

Netta holds up a finger
like she's got an idea.

She's checking the wind, distancing.
I want the room to spin.

Pity party. This is my pity party.
I want to say it out loud.

I'm living in a rented place in Mississippi,
drinking Dixie beer,

and playing the stereo loud enough
to wake the dead.

You don't know the shape I'm in.

Map Reading

In a beaten down road atlas we mark places to go,
not vacation spots, but new homes,
homes away from this one.

She uses red pen and I use blue.
She makes neat circles around town names
and I make wiggly lines around entire states.

These decisions are not entirely our own.
There is a sick father somewhere, and
there are hard feelings and money owed.

During the day Clare works. And I,
too frail from these thoughts in my head,
pop aspirin and stare at the map.

At night we lie on the bed and let
the evening warmth pour in here.
When I dream, I dream of us on that map.

I take giant steps, a hundred miles long,
a foot in Colorado and one in Utah.
At the California border my wife zigs when I zag.

Brave

If you're reading this note, I'm already gone.
That Glen Campbell song.

Another motor inn, another border town.
The king of disappointment with his last cigarette.

Wasn't I something back in the old days.
Before the world started falling down.

But that's partly a lie,
just something I say to get away smooth.

I never picked up a sword when trouble came.
I was never brave.

New Mexico

I feel like my head's going to explode.

I had a dream about you and me.

I had a dream about buying up all this sand.

I had a dream about you and me
and New Mexico.

I see the rattler by the side of the road.

I get down on my knees for one last prayer.
Let me die here,
beneath this desert air.

Driving

The spinning sound that
rejects road and asphalt
grays up at me like horizon,
blinding us on this interstate.

Shallow grooves make the tires dance,
undriven by human hands.
The music reaches us through tinted windows
of gray asphalt upon gray sky.

Yellow houses off of some unmarked state highway,
and a flag in an open, deserted field.
Grass begins to move across the feeder road,
a blade at a time.

There are cicadas in the bean fields,
calling across,
calling.

A gray ribbon of heartache and truck songs.

Rain pointing our windshield, blurring,
clouds filling the view
while wheels spill
spray up and over.

The ramp slumps from this pure gray highway,
and down into a small town
where people dwell.

A ditch,
a dirt road,
an exit sign.

The Woods

We've lived here a month,
a mile from a highway.
When I walk outside in the morning,
I see only trees.

We moved here from a big city.
You could really get around.
When we were younger,
the city was the dream.

False motion and life.
The splintered rush
of people and engagements.
A girl with headphones.

Here, just wind upon trees.
Clare touching the bark of trees.
Trees brushing back and forth in the wind.
Branch touching branch.

I motion to someone,
all of the world, maybe.

Lubbock

I bought this guitar
in a pawn shop in Amarillo.

I traded my watch
and a woman I used to know.

I say I'm from Lubbock,
but that's not it.

In fact I was born in Missouri,
trailer parks and beer halls.

I knew a woman
who traded heroes for horses.

We paid 1200 dollars for a gray El Camino.
We took turns driving, changing the plates.

Now I drink beer half the night,
until Netta comes home.

She's tender and warm.
She says, "Baby, you're all right."

Dumber Guy

Across these United States we drive.

We've been here before.
We've driven these two lanes.

Sometimes I love you so much it hurts,
other times as much as dirt.

Remember Orlando,
the bypass clear round town.

We passed up interstate
and left the hammer down.

A stranger's voice on the wire.
You left me out on the side.

You left me for a dumber guy.

Porch Swing

My memory of a giant tree branch
that showered leaves and sticks
is clouded,
not unlike the mist that falls around here.

But our porch swing,
all white slats and metal chain,
reminds me of seated sideways afternoons
and empty bottles of Tecate on the lawn.

That year in Texas,
of wicker furniture that was not ours,
of praying for rain
and huddling under the awning.

Green grass turning to brown
after first cold.
Beer bottle spinning on the road between cars.
Sound of it at night. Sound of it always at night.

Clare holding on.
The sound of the world.

Summer with the Artist

Her message is gobbledy-good,
and when I hear it
I flash on old days and the miserable
Alabama summer in the sordid mid-80s.

Smell of turpentine
and the hard scratch of canvas,
the no-doored Jeep
that served as our wedding coach.

She is two marriages down the road now,
and I'm 50 miles east or west further
away than I should be.
I suck my gut in, even on the phone.

"Can't you send me a picture,"
she says, and I stare at my free hand,
thinking of wedding bands,
thinking about the justice and his crooked tie.

Does she have my ring?
The rings of her other husbands?
Or does she melt them
into strands of gold for her hair?

Superstition Hwy.

This is a ghost town.

Best thing about it is the concrete and the asphalt.
Best thing about it is the rushing of the wheels.

This isn't heaven.

Those aren't mountains,
this isn't desert sand.

Last night I had a dream,
we were driving.
We crossed the Rio Grande.
You woke up and said, "You know,
I love Mexico."

How long must a good man run?
How fast?
How far?

Pontiac

I fell in love on the interstate.
With America and you and my 2-9-8.

100 miles and a cheap motel.
My love was pure in that Bonneville.

This is our last chance for gas.
I never loved you as much as my Pontiac.

This old car's seen better days,
and me, too, baby.

I know what I am and I'm ashamed.

Like This

I never dreamed
you'd still be waiting.

The night I left you
was sweet and cold.

I never knew "goodbye"
could mean so many miles.

We tell it like a story,
and we believe it even now.

Finally growing tired
of being who we were not.

Meet me down by the pylons.
Meet me down by the water's edge.

A Letter

Arrived in gloom of afternoon.
Rested overnight through sleep.
Opened during rainy morning.

These reachings from the past
trouble and vex regular day to day.

Shaken and unbalanced through coffee.
So thrown that my juice tastes bad, too pulpy.

Postmark had sent a guilty thrill through heart.

Hiding it from the wife not an option.
Who else do we know in Pascagoula?
She was my wife's friend first.

Clare makes grand gesture with letter opener.
Insides spill out over crumb-filled plates.
Flower petals, a Polaroid, a smeared note
with all the regular ravings.

I see across the table the reverse of the note,
the words backwards but printed bold
in child-like hand. Love, I see. Undeniable, I see.
Wife crumbles it all into one tiny fist.

Later, rain ending. Just patters of it on glass now.
Wife reading paper in the front room.
I contemplate television.

When night comes, I will take out the trash,
shrug up at heaven,
go back in.

Over You

I've got a photograph.
I carry it with me.

But it doesn't haunt me
like it once did.

Sometimes it scares me
how much she looks like you.

I'm not the same man.
But I remember.

I thought that I should let you know.

My Bad Girlfriend Blows Her Nose on My Sleeve

She fake cries at Sandy Bullock movies.

She gets her hair cut in Petaluma
(where I must drive her).
She makes me pay, and stiffs them on the tip.

She wants me to buy her lip liner, eye shadow.
She scatters pages of *Glamour* magazine
on the kitchen table.

She wears big boots and clomps
when I want to sleep.
She makes French toast and puts raspberry jam on it.

She wants to change her name to Jasmine.
She treats me to an extra-thick milkshake
then leaves lipstick on the straw.

She pulls pages out of my notebook
and fills them with terrifying poems
she says are love poems, but are clearly not.

She kisses my neighbor under the mistletoe
with an open mouth.
When she laughs, she slugs my bad arm.

She does my crossword in pen,
spelling out names of old boyfriends,
the names of her sister's cats,

and "XOXO" when nothing else fits.

Night Vision

Three wise men could find me
by the light of the television.

You could get cold here against the window,
waiting on the North Star.

I wish I had a better sense of direction,
and night vision.

Clare's out there,
beyond these rooftops.

The light from outside reaches in
and shadows me against the wall.

She will turn a corner,
see this house,

and rush in here
like madness,

like slivers from
some moon.

Driveway

It's a new haircut she comes home with.
Behind her in the trees is just the same fog.

She smiles, accidental.
Something from a happy time,
or maybe nothing at all.

A blue sweater I don't remember.
That and the haircut shake me.
I feel that as I stand on this driveway
I am seeing someone new.

Someone who hasn't seen me hollow.

It's on nights like this
the two chairs are close enough.

Underneath us the planet is spinning,
and we, like everything else,
spin along with it.

We both remark on the sky's orange color,
and how it seems different or the same
than the night before.

In a few moments she will grow tired of the quiet.
I'll watch her bedroom light go on,
and then off.

We used to go in together,
never thinking to retrieve
the lawn chairs from the rain.

Winter Afternoon

Longish curves of light soften her face.

It is nice to sit here quietly,
watching some of the afternoon
slip past us and into something else entirely.

I watch her as she gets up,
and listen as she disappears
down the hallway.

She brings me back a cup of coffee,
the top half of a carrot muffin,
and a photo from college she found.

When the door opens and closes, a rush
of freezing air comes inside.
I feel it on my feet.

Outside, the sun brilliantly plunges
into the drifts of snow.
A car door slam. Crunch of tires.

I straighten meaningless things on a table.

Best

This clock counts out hours I'd rather spend alone.
This whole town has taken every dream.

I always loved you best
when there was nowhere else to go.

I don't have
strength enough.

I'll be five hundred miles away from here.

You ask me if I love you.
I always answer yes.

But if I really do
is anybody's guess.

Cigarette Summer

I like the action,
the lighting and the initial puff.
I cough, of course. No one can avoid it.

But on a back porch in a god-forsaken town,
I smoke all summer long.
Winstons for a while, then Marlboros.

Red packages I can crush when done.
Flip the butts in tired semicircles into a bush,
or along the cobbled rock walkway.

That Clare knows nothing of it
makes it more delicious.
I could be eating pie, I think.

Great fistfuls of apple pie,
juice dripping down my chin.
The crusts discarded in plastic bags.

But instead I blow bad smoke rings
that shoot up quickly
and are caught in some summer breeze.

When she comes back
(if she comes back),
there will be hell to pay.

Someone will have to clean all of this up.

Finding Her

I don't remember it enough now.
But there was a street, and there was this place,
and we had coffee.

It was late, two in the morning,
and we sat across from each other, sleepy,
but happy to be awake, and in a place alone.

You cupped your chin with one hand,
and let the other make circles
on the table between us.

Later, in the car, we drove around in a stumbling visitor way.
Peering from the car at darkened homes.
The sound of some song on the radio.

The next morning we were standing under a shelter.
It was raining, or it had just stopped raining.
And you were talking about something, and dreamy.

I left the cover of the shelter
and started walking toward the river.
You followed. I felt your hand on my arm.

There was this river.

Return

You know how it starts.
There's this fight,
and it's not about anything,
it's about this other fight.

And then it becomes something else,
and then there's some yelling, a door slams,
you know what it's like.
There's the sound of gravel, and a car drives away.

And then the next day comes,
things are passed back and forth,
a bracelet,
a key returned.

The high drama, the grownup misery.
And then you remember.
This is kid stuff.

Left

I knew she would call.
Her hair wet,
standing in a phone booth
near a state line.

She'd say things were wrong,
but they could be fixed.

What was said could be taken back.

The phone would ring,
and if I'd fallen asleep,
I'd pick it up and speak Clare's name.

I counted the hours and looked at the map.
I closed the curtains and lay down on the carpet.

That day and the next.
I began to have trouble getting my breath.

"Get a hold of yourself," I said to myself.
"You've got to get a hold of yourself."

Every Bad Dream

The pillow where you used to lay your head.
The end table, a glass of water.
The ceiling fan, the only sound.
Another night.

A book you never read.

It's almost morning,
it's almost been a year.

The car you used to drive.
The flowers you planted.
This is our street.

The note you left,
folded and twisted around your ring.

This is the last time I'm going to read that thing.

Every bad dream I have is about you.

Years

They can pass like a whisper
or like a wind.

The thought of stopping her
was never a possibility.

Don't think I haven't played that scene
through my head a few times either.

Blocking her at the door,
dropping her car keys down the disposal.

My body between her and the outside.

I'm only telling this
so that I won't have to explain it any more.

I could tell you how many days it's been
if I felt it would help you see my side.

I have a number of stories,
and I've told them when the situation warranted.

I slept on the couch.
Is that too much?

Clare sent me a check for the car.

Guilt money, I thought.
You'd have thought somebody died.

I could have gotten down on my knees.

Anything

Van Horn, Texas.
Take-out food in white containers.

No TV.
The whole meal in the dark.

Clare moved around the room,
changing for bed, brushing her hair.

A photo of a dog
on a plastic keychain.

I just wanted to drive away.
A straight line back to where I'd been lost.

But I didn't. I kept still.
I went to sleep, her next to me.

I could move mountains.
That's what I thought.

I thought to myself that I could do anything.

Outskirts

Outside Dallas,
Clare pulled in at a Mini-Mart.
She bought Diet Coke
and little white powdered donuts.
I ate them two at a time.

We laughed about something.
I don't remember what it was,
but it was okay.
She took a drink
and gave it to me to finish.

Then something else.

She pointed to a man in a Hawaiian shirt
that billowed open at the bottom.
When the wind blew,
you could see the expanse of his stomach.

After the last donut,
she leaned toward me and kissed me full on the mouth.

It was sorrowful.
Like she was looking for something.

Like it had all gone wrong, but she was still pitching.

Swimming

Can't get the water out of my mind.
Brand new car.
Seems like my heart's on the incline.

Sunlight beats down on the road.
Blacktop starting to erode.

She's running.
She's not coming back.
The phone rings.
It's her again.

Swimming in the big river now.

Careful

Just tell me one and one is two.

We don't have to walk the floor.

When we were young,
I was salt upon your tongue,
you were rain outside my door.

Careful, we were walking on clouds.

You can make promises
until it's light.
You've mistaken
love for pride.

I won't pretend to understand.
I'll just keep standing in this rain.

Careful, now we're walking on glass.

Cherry

My arms are up in a y-shape.
I am surrounded by hardwood trees.

A cat, a stray, stares down at me blithely,
flicking a tail when I get close.

"I'm saving you," I say.
"I'm putting it right."

My arms tire.
Ridiculous.

How many exits have I missed
to get here?

It gets darker.
The yard is cool.

What is the cost of salvation?
How does one bring a cherry tree down?

How long does it take to make a new one?

Second Marriage

Clare gets married on a stormy October afternoon.
I pass in my gift and then huddle around

with strangers near the bar.
She has on an avocado dress, short, bare legs.

I stare above her head during the ceremony.
At the first wedding,

we were half mad on some lovely red wine.
Her husband shakes my hand, then clutches me close.

"It means the world to her that you came."
"Is it you?" her grandmother says, patting my hand.

"I thought you were out of the picture."
I nod at Clare as she swirls past.

I hope the nod is full of endearment and grief.
When the band plays something herky jerky,

she comes to my table, rests her hand on my shoulder.
"Just once around, okay?" she says.

A Postcard to Netta

By the time you read this I will be home.
I hope your old car is still working,
and that hose I fixed has not leaked.

There are two hundred and eleven ways
to say goodbye. Only a few will fit
on the back of this postcard.

I wish I could have stayed for another week.
Did I leave a pair of shoes there somewhere?
Was there anything we did that was fun?

I am searching for an exit line.

"I am not who anyone thought I was."

And then just my name.

My Bad Girlfriend Turns Forty

On the phone, Netta says she wants to share
some new advice she has
about yogurt, gluten, toxins.

I am visited by an image of her,
a halo of hair,
at that first party.

She cartwheeled
through the tall grass
of someone's backyard.

We've not spoken for months.
She is a year older, and then another.
I'm counting but cannot catch up.

Husband in Illinois.
Divorce in Utah.
Someone threw a hot plate.

Back then, she told me she would
wreck everything.
I made her.

I was years younger.
I loved as much
as I could, considering my reach.

While she talks, I move around my room.
I find two photographs of her.
One I stole from a wedding album.

The other we took together,
in the middle of the madness,
at a truck stop.

I remember fried chicken on the front seat,
a shithole hotel,
Bossier City, Louisiana.

Her phone buzzes.
She doesn't know what to do,
finish her story, take another call.

While she decides, I look out the window.
I see something dreamy in every cloud.

Starvation

And then there was this thing that happened,
and we didn't say anything about it.
And when it was time to go on,
I just stood outside her place
at one in the morning,
and I was on my way out of town.
The least you can do is say goodbye.

Instead I just stood there,
and I said three wishes.

I know it happened on a night
when it felt like rain,
but no rain came.
We were saying something about separations,
and the west,
and we were talking about saving lives.

And one of us,
I can't recall which one,
said it.

It was about starving,
and banana pie,
and waking up in someone else's house,
and leaving things behind,
and finding and losing,
and the lost.

And it was one of us who said it.

ABOUT THE AUTHOR

Pfefferle's first poetry collection, *The Meager Life and Modest Times of Pop Thorndale*, won the Stevens Manuscript Prize in 2007. In 2004, he published *Poets on Place*, the story of his year-long trip around America interviewing and photographing American poets in their native habitats. Pfefferle also wrote *Writing That Matters*, a college textbook. He works as a college professor, including as the past Director of Expository Writing at Johns Hopkins University, and as poetry and writing professor at Georgetown College.

He's a graduate of the Center for Writers Ph.D. program at the University of Southern Mississippi, where he worked with longtime mentor Frederick Barthelme, and earned his MFA at American University under the guidance of Henry Taylor.

His poetry has been published widely, in *Virginia Quarterly Review, Antioch Review, North American Review, Nimrod, Carolina Quarterly, Mississippi Review, Indiana Review, Greensboro Review, South Carolina Review, The Ohio Review*, and elsewhere.

Pfefferle and his wife, Beth, have been married for thirty years and have lived in nine states.

~4BMP~

ABOUT THE WORD WORKS

The Word Works, a nonprofit literary organization, publishes contemporary poetry and presents public programs.

Its publishing imprints include The Washington Prize, The Hilary Tham Capital Collection, International Editions, and The Tenth Gate Prize. A reading period is also held in May.

Monthly, The Word Works offers free literary programs in the Chevy Chase, MD, Café Muse series, and each summer, it holds free poetry programs in Washington, DC's Rock Creek Park. Annually in June, two high school students debut in the Joaquin Miller Poetry Series as winners of the Jacklyn Potter Young Poets Competition. Since 1974, Word Works programs have included: "In the Shadow of the Capitol," a symposium and archival project on the African American intellectual community in segregated Washington, DC; the Gunston Arts Center Poetry Series; the Poet Editor panel discussions at The Writer's Center; and Master Class workshops.

As a 501(c)3 organization, The Word Works has received awards from the National Endowment for the Arts, the National Endowment for the Humanities, the D.C. Commission on the Arts & Humanities, the Witter Bynner Foundation, Poets & Writers, The Writer's Center, Bell Atlantic, the David G. Taft Foundation, and others, including many generous private patrons.

The Word Works has established an archive of artistic and administrative materials in the Washington Writing Archive housed in the George Washington University Gelman Library. It is a member of the Council of Literary Magazines and Presses and its books are distributed by Small Press Distribution.

More information at WordWorksBooks.org.

OTHER WORD WORKS BOOKS

Karren L. Alenier, *Wandering on the Outside*
Karren L. Alenier, Hilary Tham, Miles David Moore, eds.,
    Winners: A Retrospective of the Washington Prize
Christopher Bursk, ed., *Cool Fire*
Barbara Goldberg, *Berta Broadfoot and Pepin the Short*
Jacklyn Potter, Dwaine Rieves, Gary Stein, eds.,
    Cabin Fever: Poets at Joaquin Miller's Cabin
Robert Sargent, *Aspects of a Southern Story*
    & A Woman From Memphis

THE TENTH GATE PRIZE

Lisa Sewell, *Impossible Object*, 2014

INTERNATIONAL EDITIONS

Keyne Cheshire (trans.), *Murder at Jagged Rock:*
    A Tragedy by Sophocles
Yoko Danno & James C. Hopkins, *The Blue Door*
Moshe Dor, Barbara Goldberg, Giora Leshem, eds.,
    The Stones Remember
Moshe Dor (Barbara Goldberg, trans.), *Scorched by the Sun*
Lee Sang (Myong-Hee Kim, trans.), *Crow's Eye View:*
    The Infamy of Lee Sang, Korean Poet
Vladimir Levchev (Henry Taylor, trans.), *Black Book of the*
    Endangered Species

WASHINGTON PRIZE BOOKS

Nathalie F. Anderson, *Following Fred Astaire*, 1998
Michael Atkinson, *One Hundred Children Waiting
    for a Train*, 2001
Molly Bashaw, *The Whole Field Still Moving Inside It*, 2013
Carrie Bennett, *biography of water*, 2004
Peter Blair, *Last Heat*, 1999
John Bradley, *Love-in-Idleness: The Poetry of Roberto
    Zingarello*, 1995, 2nd edition, 2015
Richard Carr, *Ace*, 2008
Jamison Crabtree, *Rel[AM]ent*, 2014
B. K. Fischer, *St. Rage's Vault*, 2012
Ann Rae Jonas, *A Diamond Is Hard But Not Tough*, 1997
Frannie Lindsay, *Mayweed*, 2009
Richard Lyons, *Fleur Carnivore*, 2005
Fred Marchant, *Tipping Point*, 1993, 2nd edition 2013
Ron Mohring, *Survivable World*, 2003
Brad Richard, *Motion Studies*, 2010
Jay Rogoff, *The Cutoff*, 1994
Prartho Sereno, *Call from Paris*, 2007, 2nd edition 2013
Enid Shomer, *Stalking the Florida Panther*, 1987
John Surowiecki, *The Hat City after Men Stopped Wearing
    Hats*, 2006
Miles Waggener, *Phoenix Suites*, 2002
Mike White, *How to Make a Bird with Two Hands*, 2011
Nancy White, *Sun, Moon, Salt*, 1992, 2nd edition 2010

www.ingramcontent.com/pod-product-compliance
Lightning Source LLC
Chambersburg PA
CBHW031007090426

42737CB00008B/713